BRUCE THE GOOSE

Operetta in Two Acts

Music & Libretto by
Sean M McGowan

Ed. 1

Bruce The Goose

Copyright 2020, All The Musicals

All rights of any kind, including but not limited to stage, radio, television, performance, motion picture, mechanical, printing, and selling, are strictly reserved. License to perform this work in whole or in part must be secured in writing from All The Musicals.

To perform this show, go to **allthemusicals.com** and you'll be up and running in no time.

The Story

Act I

It's Election Day. Bea the Bee dutifully circles the Lake of Lakes, the Home of a Hundred Species. She calls one animal from every species to the Grand Assembly, where all official Lake business is decided by democratic vote. But this year, something's different. Bruce the Goose wants to replace the Grand Assembly with his own unchallenged authority. After a vigorous debate, Scout the Trout casts the deciding vote and elects Bruce, plunging the Lake into a fascist dictatorship.

Act II

One year later, the Lake is a sad dystopia. Everyone's been drafted into Bruce's army. As they prepare to invade the Next Lake Over, it becomes clear to everyone that Bruce has lost his mind – that his vanity and pride keep him from serving the public interest. Bruce's lust for war medals weighs him down so much he sinks to the bottom of the Lake. Everyone realizes Bruce is gone and decides to bring back the Grand Assembly. They hold another Election Day, restoring the Lake to a democracy.

Bruce The Goose

Cast of Characters

- **BRUCE THE GOOSE** - Alto. A charismatic, ambitious diva who only cares about himself.
- **PUCK THE DUCK** - Soprano. A wise, prudent, humble steward who cares about everyone. She wears a flat cap.
- **BEA THE BEE** - Alto. An anxious, hard-working, always-busy journalist with integrity. She wears a press hat and carries reporter's journal and pencil.
- **EARL THE SQUIRREL** - Soprano. A nervous, frightened, paranoid father who believes anything he's told. He wears a knit cap.
- **SCOUT THE TROUT** - Alto. An upright, decent veteran who has to struggle just to survive. She wears a dixie cup hat.
- **CHORUS** (*optional*) - Sopranos and altos. A variety of animals from the Lake, each of a different species (such as **WORM, MOSQUITO, ANT, BUTTERFLY**), and each with a different job at the Lake (such as doctor, carpenter, chef, astronaut).

TIME: Present day
PLACE: Sloan's Lake, Denver

Synopsis of Scenes

Prologue	7
Act I	7
Scene 1 - Election Day	7
Scene 2 - The Debate	8
Scene 3 - Only Me	10
Act II	11
Scene 1 - No Elections Today	11
Scene 2 - Bruce Is Great	12
Scene 3 - Long Live The King	12
Scene 4 - Election Day (Reprise)	13

Bruce The Goose

Prologue

BEA: Sing the song that takes place on the Lake of Lakes
where the Home of a Hundred Species lives.
Sing the song about a bird who flies too high,
only to sink deep beneath the waves.
Sing the song about democracy and fascism.
Sing the song about the rise and fall of Bruce the Goose.

Act I

(Sunrise. Bea cheerfully circles the Lake, calling one animal from every species to join her at the Grand Assembly.)

Scene 1 - Election Day

BEA: Today is Election Day. Celebrate.
Everyone gather together 'cause it's a democracy we keep.
(Puck enters, greets Bea.)
Hello, my friend. It is great to see you.
I'm coming down with election fever.
Here in the Home of a Hundred Species.

PUCK, BEA (*cheerfully march together*):
One representative from every one.
It's Election Day. Celebrate.
Everyone gather together 'cause it's a democracy. A lot to see.
One vote for everyone under the sun. It's Election Day today.

EARL (*enters, greets everyone*):
Hello, my friends. I am getting nervous.
Doing my best but my kids are hurting.
Gathering nuts is an awful burden.

EARL, PUCK, BEA (*cheerfully march together*):
Maybe today we will change it
because it's Election Day today.

SCOUT (*enters, greets everyone*):
Hello, my friends. So, it's now up to us
because I've got a list of complaints for the public.
Our system was built to reward the injustice.

PUCK, BEA, EARL, SCOUT (*cheerfully march together*):
So, everyone stand up for everyone else.
It's Election Day. Celebrate.
Everyone gather together 'cause it's a democracy. A lot to see.
Now is the day that we speak and we listen to everyone. Lots of fun.

One vote for everyone under the sun. It's Election Day today.

BRUCE (*enters, greets no one*):
>It is I, Bruce the Goose.
>And I alone can lead you on:
>Scout the Trout, Earl the Squirrel,
>Bea the Bee, and even Puck the Duck.

PUCK *(to Bea)*:
>What's with him?

BEA: He's on the ballot.

PUCK *(to Bruce)*: Well, good luck!

(*Bruce yawns, amuses himself while the others cheerfully march on.*)

ALL *(except Bruce)*:
>Today is Election Day. Celebrate.
>Everyone gather together 'cause it's a democracy. A lot to see.
>Now is the day that we speak and we listen to everyone. Lots of fun.
>One vote for everyone under the sun. It's Election Day today.
>One vote for everyone under the sun. It's Election Day today.

Scene 2 - The Debate

(***Everyone gathers in Assembly at the East End of the Lake. Bruce drags his feet, doesn't pay attention, is the last to join.***)

BEA: Welcome, today's Grand Assembly of One Hundred Species, where everyone votes. And the first on the docket's the presidency.

BRUCE: No, no, no. I'm running for king.

BEA: No, the only position's for president.

BRUCE: I will change the rules. I alone can fix it, and that's what I'll do as your king.

BEA: Ahem. I call us to order today, in an orderly fashion, let's...

BRUCE: No, no, no. The media's lying to you.

BEA: So, let's now begin the debate between our two

	candidates, then we can
	vote. Ahem.
	So, what will you do about
	the media?
	And do you believe in our freedom of speech?
	Puck the Duck?
PUCK:	We will
	fight to protect
	our freedom of the press, and of journalists.
	That's what we'll do.
BEA:	Bruce the Goose?
BRUCE:	I will
	end the news.
	I'll tell the truth
	myself.
	That's what I'll do.
EARL:	What will you do about the children?
	My babies need care while I'm gathering nuts.
	Bruce the Goose?
BRUCE:	I will
	close the schools
	enlist your children
	to fight with us.
	That's what I'll do
	as your king.
EARL:	Puck the Duck?
PUCK:	We will
	fight to protect
BRUCE:	No, you won't.
PUCK:	our teachers and schools, for the children.
	That's what we'll do.
SCOUT:	And what will you do about
	elections?
	And do you believe we should all have a vote?
	Puck the Duck?
PUCK:	We will
	fight to perfect
BRUCE:	No, no, no.
PUCK:	our imperfect democracy
	and things will improve.
SCOUT:	Bruce the Goose?
BRUCE:	I will
	end the vote
	and fix all your problems

BRUCE:	myself. That's what I'll do, so, elect me your king. I alone can fix it. Only I can make us great, and lead us into a glorious Lake. So, choose me and give me control of your destiny. So, let's cast the vote.	**PUCK:**	You'll tear us apart and divide us in two. Here, we work together. It's not only you who can fight to protect our right to elect our own leaders. That's why we choose to vote for ourselves, take control of our destiny. So, let's cast the vote.

BRUCE (*stands stage left*):
    Bruce the Goose.
PUCK (*stands stage right*):
    Puck the Duck.
EARL (*stands stage left*):
    Bruce the Goose.
BEA (*stands stage right*):
    Puck the Duck.
SCOUT (*stands stage left*):
    Bruce the Goose.

Scene 3 - Only Me

BRUCE (*crowns himself*):
    When I was young, I knew I'd fly to higher heights
    above the sky, beyond where any bird has flown.
    But now I'm grown and I'm the only one who's seen the light,
    that only I was chosen as the chosen one.
    Only me. Only me.
    I alone will tell the truth when the fake media lies.
    Only I will tell the truth when others won't.
    I alone can fix the problems in society.
    Only I can heal all our country's wounds.
    Only me. Only me.
    Only me. Only me.
    I alone can keep you safe from the other side.
    Only I can keep you safe inside your home.
    I alone can protect you in the wars to come.
    And only I can save your everlasting souls.
    Only me. Only me.
    Only me. Only me.
    Only me.

Act II

(One year later. Sunset. The Lake is a sad dystopia.)

Scene 1 - No Elections Today

BEA (*alone on the Lake*):
>A year has gone by since the last Election Day.
>A year has gone by in pain.
>There's no democracy since Bruce became our king.
>There's no elections today.

(Puck enters.)

PUCK, BEA: I remember the greatness of
>the Hundred Species as one.
>There's no democracy since Bruce became our king.
>There's no elections today.

EARL (*enters*): I'm falling apart 'cause I can't feed my kids.
>I'm struggling just to live.
>There's no one to talk to about my pain.
>There's no elections today.

(Scout enters.)

EARL, SCOUT:
>I'm falling apart 'cause I struggle
>just to survive.
>I'm falling apart 'cause there's no way to change.
>There's no elections today.

PUCK, BEA: A year has gone by since the last Election Day.
EARL, SCOUT: I'm falling apart 'cause I can't feed my kids.
PUCK, BEA: A year has gone by in pain.
EARL, SCOUT: I'm struggling just to live.
PUCK, BEA: There's no democracy since Bruce became our king.
EARL, SCOUT: There's no one to talk to about my pain.
PUCK, BEA, EARL, SCOUT:
>There's no elections today.
PUCK, BEA: I remember the greatness of
EARL, SCOUT: I'm falling apart 'cause I struggle
PUCK, BEA: the Hundred Species as one.
EARL, SCOUT: just to survive.
PUCK, BEA: There's no democracy since Bruce became our king.
EARL, SCOUT: I'm falling apart 'cause there's no way to change.
PUCK, BEA, EARL, SCOUT:
>There's no elections today.

Scene 2 - Bruce Is Great

BRUCE (*enters, furious*):
    What? Singing?
    Sing no songs unless they glorify the Lake of Lakes,
    unless they honor a great patriot like me.
    Sing no songs unless they lionize our warriors
    and enshrine our infallible king.
    Sing no songs unless you sing them for a thousand years
    and immortalize all my victories.
    (***leads everyone in a march to the West End of the Lake***)
    Like this. Sopranos.

SOPRANOS: Bruce is great. Bruce is glorious.
    Bruce will keep us safe.
    We will be victorious
    because Bruce is great.

BRUCE: No, no, no. It must be more patriotic.
    Like this. Altos.

ALTOS (*except Bruce*):
    Bruce is great. Bruce is glorious.
    Bruce will keep us safe.
    We will be victorious
    because Bruce is great.

BRUCE: No, no, no. It must have more zeal.
    Like this. All together now.

ALL (*Except Bruce*):
    Bruce is great. Bruce is glorious.
    Bruce will keep us safe.
    We will be victorious
    because Bruce is great.

BRUCE: Terrible. Just terrible.
    We'll work on it.

Scene 3 - Long Live The King

    (***Everyone gathers in Assembly at the West End. Bruce swims out in front of everyone.***)

BRUCE: Earl, bring me my
    war medals, war medals.

    (***Earl nervously pins Bruce's war medals on him. With each medal, Bruce sinks a little deeper into the Lake.***)

BRUCE: Long live the king.
    More medals. More medals. More medals.
    Into the breach, my soldiers. Some of you will not survive
    and we'll sing songs about your glorious demise.

Into the breach to make the ultimate sacrifice
for your king, as long as I'm alive.
Long live the king. More medals.
Long live the king. More medals.
Into the breach, my subjects. Onward to the vast abyss
for the glory of your all-glorious king.
Into the breach. Into the darkness of the great beyond.
Into the light of your everlasting soul.
Long live the king.
Long live the king.
Long live the king.
Long li–

(Bruce sinks beneath the Lake. Earl goes to help, but Scout gently restrains him. Bruce dies.)

ALL: So is the end
of Bruce the Goose.

Scene 4 - Election Day (Reprise)

(Everyone looks at each other, tries to decide what to do next.)

BEA: So, who will decide, now that Bruce is gone,
decide which direction the Lake is on?

EARL: The Home of a Hundred Species needs

PUCK: a forum to settle our disagreements.

(Scout gets an idea.)

SCOUT: Finally, my friends, so it's all up to us because

SCOUT, BEA: we've got a list of complaints for the public.

SCOUT, EARL, BEA:
Our system was built to reward the injustice.

ALL: So everyone stand up for everyone else.
It's Election Day. Celebrate.
Everyone gather together 'cause it's a democracy. A lot to see.
Now is the day that we speak and we listen to everyone. Lots of fun.
One vote for everyone under the sun. It's Election Day today.
One vote for everyone under the sun. It's Election Day today.

(End of the operetta.)

Vocal Score

Prologue

Election Day

The Debate

MUSIC & LYRICS BY
SEAN M MCGOWAN

77.2564 BPM

BEA
Wel- come, to- day's Grand As- sem- bly of One Hun- dred Spe- cies, where eve- ry- one votes. And the first on the do- cket's the pre- si-den- cy.

BRUCE
No, no, no. I'm run- ning for king.

BEA
No, the

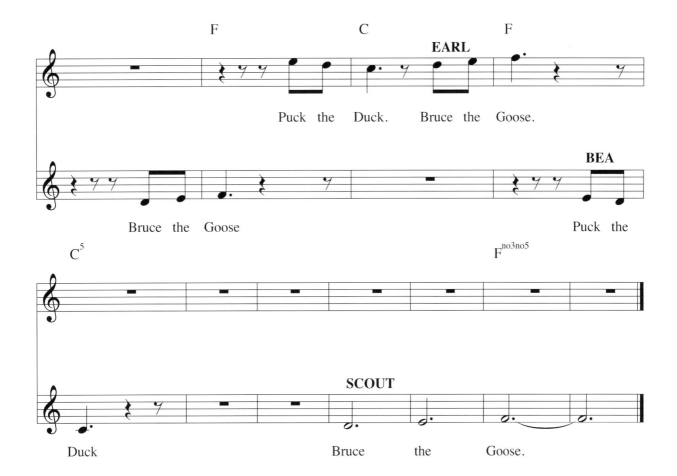

Only Me

81.8503 BPM

MUSIC & LYRICS BY
SEAN M MCGOWAN

BRUCE

When I was young, I knew I'd fly to hi- gher heights a- bove the sky, be- yond where a- ny bird has flo- o- own. But now I'm grown and I'm the on- ly one who's seen the light, that on- ly I was cho- sen as the cho- sen o- o- one. On- ly me. On- ly me. I a- lone will tell the truth when the fake me- di- a lies. On- ly I will tell the truth when o- thers wo- o- on't. I a-

No Elections Today

Bruce Is Great

Election Day (Reprise)

Made in the USA
Columbia, SC
27 May 2021